THE MANTLE OF PURITY

by

Julie Brown

Grosvenor House
Publishing Limited

First Edition – April 2018

The right of Julie Brown to be identified as the author of this
work has been asserted in accordance with Section 78
of the Copyright, Designs and Patents Act 1988

The book cover picture is copyright to Julie Brown

This book is published by
Grosvenor House Publishing Ltd
Link House
140 The Broadway, Tolworth, Surrey, KT6 7HT.
www.grosvenorhousepublishing.co.uk

Julie Brown can be contacted at info@thebridalcompany.org
Her ministry website is: www.thebridalcompany.org

A CIP record for this book
is available from the British Library

ISBN 978-1-78623-178-9

DEDICATION

To my beloved Parents, Ian and Margaret
&
My Spiritual Parents, Jim and Cynthia Wilkinson

Heroes of the Faith
and God's Most Precious Gift to Me

TABLE OF CONTENTS

ACKNOWLEDGEMENTS

I would like to honour the people God has used to bless and strengthen my walk with Him, through all these years: My parents, Ian and Margaret Brown and my spiritual parents, Jim and Cynthia Wilkinson. David & Florence Brown, West House Christian Fellowship. Ed & Ruth Silvoso and the entire Harvest Evangelism Team. Arthur Burke, Sapphire Leadership Group. Ken & Lois Gott, for the life-changing conferences they hosted during the 'Times of Refreshing' in the 90's. David & Carol Tattersall, Generation Ministries International. Johnny Foote, Flame of Fire International and Liz Wright, The Bridal Company.

Thank you, for paying a price I did not have to in order to receive from the fruit you bear in your walk with God. My life has been eternally changed because of you.

I would also like to honour all of the people who have sown into my ministry for over twenty years. I would especially like to thank Margaret Brown, Jill Brown, Ross & Lynne Whitehill, Robbie and Sue Coull,

Tony Manning, Les Trewinnard, Hollybush Christian Fellowship and Tommy and Lulu de Mallet Morgan for their faithful support particularly in the last few years. I have walked by faith and the miracle of sovereign provision is my experience. Every single supporter has played an integral role as the way has supernaturally opened up before me for over two decades and the testimony contained in the pages of this book would not have been possible without you. I thank each one of you, from the bottom of my heart.

I am grateful to William and Karen Porter for their incredible ministry 'Beacon House of Prayer' in Stoke on Trent, the setting in which the encounter which has become the heart of this book, took place. The faithful and tireless commitment to 24/7 prayer and worship upheld by the entire Beacon team is producing fruit of eternal value.

Thank you to those who have cheered me on as I wrote my first book! Jill Elizabeth, my darling Sister, what an example and beautiful gift from God you are to me. My Mum, my beloved and courageous friend. Liz Wright, a shining champion of the faith. June Brown, a pillar in the Temple of our God. Gina Cooke, a far-seeing woman of great stature in the Kingdom. Kim Cross, a man who stands by appointment at the crossroads and makes things happen for God! Ross and Lynne Whitehill, my friends for life and Oliver Pengilly, the gifted and anointed artist who so beautifully painted the cover for this book.

To God be the Glory!

FOREWORD

LIZ WRIGHT

As the vision of Heaven's Throne Room opened up before me, I watched as thousands upon thousands of the great multitude began to cry out in one accord, "It is FINISHED, it is FINISHED!" Their powerful declaration thundered through my spirit and began to move out to touch the Body of Christ worldwide!

Understanding was released to me that the message of the Gospel in its purest form will be understood again, in our generation. THE MESSAGE OF THE CROSS is coming back centre-stage and with it, the power to live from Golgotha's finished work, enabling us to experience the 'new creation reality.'

We will fully understand the glorious reality of the Mystical Union, Christ IN us. The very core of our nature and strength becoming the uncreated substance of God Himself.

As Jesus hung on the cross He entered into covenant with us. Crying out, 'It is Finished', the Aramaic word he used was 'Hallah', which means 'Bride', 'the one I have cut covenant with.' As His Holy Spirit then poured into those made new by His blood, His 'Hallah' became a living being! A people made in His exact likeness, perfected in holiness, reflecting his beauty, glory and power, united in the 'Mystical Union' to love and transform a world lost in darkness.

As Julie shares with us in this powerful book, a Bridal Company is emerging in the earth, awakened to the reality of who we really are in Christ: a people living from the place of IT IS FINISHED, tasting the inner freedom and joy that the early church knew.

Through the account of her extraordinary journey with God, she testifies to the truth that with each encounter, because of our one-ness with the indwelling Spirit of God, we see with unveiled faces the truth of who we really are. We are made in the exact likeness of God and have been given power to completely align with the Truth that sets us free!

Julie and I have done life together for 15 years. She is one of the greatest treasures of my life. Our friendship is a gift from Heaven, as we've laughed and cried through the many seasons, with one thing as our primary focus: knowing Jesus and learning how to live life abiding in Him.

I have the privilege of knowing first-hand that every word in this book is true. It is the testimony of Jesus as

He has enfolded Julie in His love, activating her into her highest calling: to walk as His Bride!

There is therefore an invitation to you right now, to enter in, to go deeper. To see who you really are and live in the freedom that is yours in Christ. No matter what you are going through, Jesus is reaching out to you and inviting you to take hold of his hand. He wants to show you how to live as His New Creation, the Second Eve, clothed in the Mantle of Purity!

Liz Wright, Co-Founder and Senior Director
The Bridal Company

INTRODUCTION

Just one day after returning to live in England, on October 23rd 2002, I received a word from a Prophet, Johnny Foote[1], at the Houses of Parliament, London. For the previous four years I had been living in San Jose, California, serving in ministry with Ed Silvoso and Harvest Evangelism when God placed a sovereign call on my life to the destiny of my home nation. Within 24 hours of coming home, this man of God spoke many wonderful things directly into my life, confirming Father's intention to restore England's broken gates and walls, to revive our people and our land. He also prophesied that I would write:

"Sister, one of the things you are going to begin doing is writing out. Writing out liberty. Go ahead, get the paper, get the pen, get it going, because He is going to give you the ink and it is going to be fulfilled. The ministry is come and it is upon you, for the Lord's anointing is upon you. It is not refreshing the Body,

---

[1] Johnny Foote, Flame of Fire International, Pensacola, Florida

many are there to refresh, but the Lord says, "I have called you by appointment, to stand with Me. There are days of standing, days of coming into My House and as you come and stand in your position with Me, now write. As you write, you will write in detail, of what is key and what is not key. I have trained you and I have schooled you to write out liberty, even unto the nations. You shall declare for Me, you shall know the heart of my heart and this shall be the writing of that, of the Lamb. You shall write for Me, you shall declare, for the detail is the heart of my heart."

Even though I was born again as a 9 year-old girl and God had graciously filled my life with rich blessings and experiences in His Presence, the prophetic word I have just shared with you contained a promise so deep, to know the heart of the Lamb, that I treasured it very deeply in my heart. The wondrous promise of love and deep fellowship with Jesus became a 'life word' that sustained me through many challenging years that followed. I literally read and re-read the prophetic word hundreds of times, feeling the love of Jesus reaching out, helping me to rest, to lay my head upon His breast as John did and in time, this led to an invitation that went deeper still...

There is joy in my heart to release this first book and my prayer as we walk through these pages together, reading the words I'm writing from my heart, is that there will be an impartation from the Holy Spirit and you will be touched deep in *your* heart by the King. Whether you have known God for decades or just for a short time, there is an invitation for you, to begin a new journey that will take you deep into the very depths of His Presence.

God promised me that I would stand in my position beside Him and then release the details, of what is key and what is not key and it is my testimony that even though I am anointed as a prophetic strategist in intercession, the greatest key of all is to pursue one thing and one thing alone: a personal and loving relationship with Jesus.

Your desire, love and appreciation for Him as a Person will release into your life all of the love that is *in* Him, providing you with the power you need to achieve breakthrough in every single area of life! Jesus is the key and it is His heartbeat to reveal Himself and make Himself known to those who love Him:

"The person who has My commands and keeps them is
the one who [really] loves Me;
and whoever loves Me will be loved by My Father
and I too will love him and will
show [reveal and manifest] Myself to him.
[I will let Myself be clearly seen by him and
make Myself real to him.]" John 14:21

ROOTS

Where does the power come from, to experience the reality of who Jesus is and then live for Him?

My family discovered the answer to this question in the late 1960's as my father received a promotion that would move us from our coastal home in Sunderland to farming country in North Yorkshire. Young and full of dreams, my parents embraced this new beginning never thinking for a moment that they were about to encounter the power of the Holy Spirit in their lives!

As their home stubbornly refused to sell, Dad began his new job anyway, arriving one day at Hollybush Farm near Thirsk to sell some agricultural oils. Greeted at the door by the farmer, Jim Wilkinson, business was soon completed but something much more important began to unfold as Jim, the leader of a small fellowship of Christians meeting at the farm, gave my Dad a word of knowledge, "Your house will be sold by the end of the week" he said, extending an invitation to come anytime to the weekly meetings being held at Hollybush House. Driving away Dad laughed to himself, "How could he know our house will sell?" and more uncomfortably for him, he pondered "How could he know anything about me and my faith?"

As the week drew to a close, Dad returned to Sunderland to find that indeed, the house was sold. Within weeks his little family took up residence much further away from those north-east roots than they had planned for, settling in the market town of Northallerton, just 5 miles from Hollybush Farm. God has a way of getting us exactly where He wants us to be.

My Mum, Margaret, had been soundly born again at 14 in a mission to an impoverished council estate in the heart of Sunderland and Dad had a Christian upbringing, attending church all of his life. As they took up Jim Wilkinson's offer however and attended their first 'fellowship' meeting at Hollybush House, neither of them were prepared for the impact of the vibrant praise, the strange language people were using, the powerful prayers and preaching that seemed to grip their hearts in a way they had never known. This was not church as they knew it, there was an intensity about the way these people related to God and not knowing how to respond, unable to find any familiar ground on which to stand, they walked out.

What did these people have that they did not they wondered? The zeal and enthusiasm for God that they had witnessed in the meeting only seemed to highlight the absence of such a fire in their own hearts and it was very provoking, particularly for my Mum. Dad was less interested. Within days however, they were drawn in a manner that could not be explained, to go back to the farm and so began their attendance at Hollybush Christian Fellowship.[2]

Jim and Cynthia Wilkinson were Yorkshire farmers with deep roots in Methodism. They had been heavily involved in local church, spending much of their spare time in reaching people with the Gospel and then they themselves had been transformed by the powerful baptism of the Holy Spirit under the ministry of George Breckon. Their lives were radically changed and revival began to break out as weekly meetings for fellowship and teaching were soon underway in their home.

The power of the Holy Spirit flowed freely. The gifts of the Spirit were encouraged and relied upon, the opportunity to receive this 'infilling of the Spirit' offered in such a way that it was impossible to avoid, bringing nearly everyone that came into those meetings into a vibrant and living relationship with Jesus Christ. One by one the people came: Christians and total unbelievers, old and young, denomination by denomination, the curious, the sceptical, the broken and the demonised. This incredible couple, Jim and Cynthia, opened up the very heart of their own home to host the presence of God and allow 'whosoever will' to come and receive of the Spirit's power and anointing in their lives. Countless numbers have come to this well ever since and found a water to drink that never will run dry.

---

[2] The full story of Hollybush Christian Fellowship is told in 'Miracle Valley', © Jim Wilkinson with Chris Spencer, first published in 1984 by Marshall, Morgan & Scott, Updated & Re-published in 2001, Harvey Wilkinson Publishers

This is where my Dad, Ian Brown, was wonderfully born-again, where he and my Mum were baptized in the Holy Spirit with such power that they were transformed and never lost their fire. This is where the power of God was made manifest to them as they witnessed countless miracles: the sick being healed, the demonised being set free, those in the grip of the occult being liberated, miracle provision of all kinds poured into the laps of those who needed it. This is where my family and thousands of others discovered that the power to experience the reality of who Jesus is, the power to live in Him and for Him, comes from the third person of the Trinity. The glorious Holy Spirit.

What truths our family learned from those years at Hollybush, as fresh and relevant today as they were nearly 50 years ago because these truths are eternal. Distinct in the Godhead, we learned that the Holy Spirit is the POWER of the Lord and that He is the very basis of our life in Jesus. He is our connection to the Godhead, responsible for our new birth in Christ. Jesus revealed His vital ministry as he spoke to Zacchaeus:

"Most assuredly, I say to you, unless one is born of water and the Spirit he cannot enter the Kingdom of God" John 3:5 NKJV

We have all had a physical birth (born of water) but to see, enter and carry the Kingdom of God within us, we must have a spiritual birth, being born of the Spirit, which literally means to be born 'of God' because the source of our new birth is God Himself. The Spirit unites us to the Person of Jesus Christ, we become part of His Body and our new life is rooted in Him, in the immoveable security of the love of the Father. What an incredible truth this is for us!

Our new life 'born of the Spirit' is the abundant, eternal life Jesus died to give us and becoming 'born again' is just the beginning. We have a unique, God-given destiny to fulfil and as the Spirit helps, teaches and empowers us, our carnal nature is transformed until we:

> "*Come to a knowledge of the Son of God, to a perfect man, to the measure of the stature of the fullness of Christ.*" Ephesians 4:13

We are to become like Jesus Himself. In the wisdom of God's plan of salvation, *our* calling and destiny is to become like Jesus, filled to overflowing with His love, nature and power, carrying His Presence into every sphere of society and every sphere of influence.

To live this new life, we need the power of the Spirit filling our lives every moment of every day. We need the on-going infilling of the Spirit to receive the *power* to become like Jesus, filled with His love and authority, bearing the fruit of the Spirit and operating in the gifts of the Spirit so that we may do the greater works that He prophesied we would do. Jesus knew as He returned to the right hand of His Father, that the twelve apostles *needed* the Spirit's power in order to fulfil their ministry calling and promised that He would send His Spirit to be that source of power, fellowship and counsel among them:

"But you shall receive power when the Holy Spirit has come upon you; and you shall be witnesses to Me in Jerusalem and in all Judea and Samaria and to the ends of the earth." Acts 1: 8 NKJV

It is no different for us. We too need to be daily filled with the same power in order to fulfil Jesus' call upon *our* lives and this power comes from the third person of the Trinity: the precious Holy Spirit.

Benny Hinn's ground-breaking book, 'Good Morning Holy Spirit' movingly describes the Holy Spirit as a beautiful and sensitive, yet powerful Person, highlighting His unique ministry to glorify Jesus Christ the Son of God. Only Jesus is glorified in a life that is filled with the Spirit.[3]

The more you seek Jesus, the more you know that the Spirit is dwelling within you, giving you the power to know Jesus personally. The more like Jesus you become, the more you know that you are receiving the Spirit's power because the true transformation process of our soul cannot to be achieved in our strength but in HIS.

Ephesians 1:22-23 lays before us our life's vision, no matter what your personal calling may be:

"And He put all things under His feet and gave Him to be Head over all things to the Church (Ekklesia), which is His Body, the fullness of Him who fills all in all."

---

[3] 'Good Morning Holy Spirit', paraphrased from Page 60, © Benny Hinn 1990, Thomas Nelson Publishers

Jesus is filling everything, everywhere with Himself, through us. The power of God has been made freely available to us by the Spirit, enabling us to fulfil this incredible calling, literally being transformed from glory to glory, our old carnal nature being replaced by His perfect nature as we go deeper and deeper into Jesus, who is hidden in the Father.

This is the new life we have been born into. Just as Mary was overshadowed by the Spirit of God and brought forth Jesus, the Son of God, we too have been overshadowed and infilled with *the same Spirit*, to bring forth the character and nature of Jesus Himself, that we might manifest His Presence and His Kingdom everywhere we go.

This is the experience my parents came into at Hollybush. This is the power that they found to know Jesus in a vibrant new way. Set in the midst as a little child, the imprint of the memory of the presence of the Lord, made manifest to me by the power of the Holy Spirit, was set irrevocably upon my own spirit. Sewn like a golden thread into the fabric of my life, indelible and resident within, the Holy Spirit proved His ministry to me, providing me with the power to know Jesus in a very real way. This inheritance would direct the course of the rest of my life.

FACE TO FACE

As the years unfolded, our family moved from Yorkshire to Lincolnshire and I started out life as a young adult. Having taken a few wrong turns away from the Lord, the precious memory of knowing Jesus so personally faded a little from view, but in the early 80's by God's grace my heart was drawn to commit to Him in a decision that was final. I began to diligently pursue God's call upon my life, serving in local church, volunteering with Youth for Christ and taking my first steps towards ministry training with YWAM in 1991. Inwardly and unconsciously however, I was trying to find the powerful connection to Jesus that I'd known and witnessed years before.

In 1993 after a particularly difficult year, as I read Benny Hinn's book, "Good Morning Holy Spirit" the Spirit began to minister directly to me, revitalising my weary heart as the power I was searching for started to touch my life once again.

Benny's account of the Spirit's ministry and presence was gripping. Describing Him as a mighty, yet gentle, childlike person that wants to stay close to those who love Him, Benny asks the question: how was it that Charles Finney could preach the Gospel and people would be 'slain under the power', confessing their sins? Or what was the power that fell when John Wesley opened his mouth to preach? Why would kitchen staff at a convention centre fall to the ground as Kathryn Kuhlman passed them by? He answered those wonderful questions with a profound statement: **it was the person of the Holy Spirit that accompanied their ministry.**[4]

The more I read, as an adult now, the more I longed to have the reality of relationship with the Holy Spirit that Benny and Kathryn Kuhlman had. The fresh understanding that the Spirit is a Person you can get to know, impacted me deeply and a whole new realm of potential was opened up as I read of the fruit that such a relationship brought! It was another milestone on the journey.

In the early 90's 'Times of Refreshing' hit the UK churches as we heard of the move of God in Toronto, Brownsville and Argentina and we pursued them with all of our might. It was a unique and authentic time of renewal for us as we Brits travelled to these wells and drank deeply, so deeply that we truly were 'drunk' in the Spirit. Moves of God sprang up all over our islands and we got healed, envisioned and freed up in every area of life as a result. Drawn like a magnet to what God was doing, I came under an anointing from the Spirit that

---

[4] 'Good Morning Holy Spirit', paraphrased from Page 54 & 55 © Benny Hinn 1990, Thomas Nelson Publishers

propelled me into a single- minded focus on His Presence and from that time on, nothing else would satisfy.

Memorably for me, in July 1996 Claudio Freidzon from 'Rey de Reyes' church in Belgrano, Buenos Aires came to Sunderland for a weekend conference hosted by Ken and Lois Gott. Claudio brought his family with him and their example alone would have been enough to convince me once and for all of a powerful truth that I had learned at home and from Jim and Cynthia Wilkinson, that vibrant and powerful relationship with God in the context of a deeply united and loving family is His Plan for us. Out of such a setting abundant fruit flourishes and is evident for all to see.

Claudio ministered so powerfully that weekend, demonstrating a level of authority and power in the Spirit sufficient to touch almost everyone in the room. And we were touched. It was awesome to see so many people surrendering to the tangible presence of God, thirsting to know Jesus as never before and it was impossible not to be completely in awe of the purity and power of such a ministry. As I looked upon this example, completely inspired and with longing in my heart, Jesus spoke to me from Matthew 13:44

"Again, the Kingdom of Heaven is like treasure hidden in a field, which a man found and hid and for joy over it he goes and sells all that he has and buys that field."

I knew I had found my treasure hidden in the field and Jesus was gently telling me that it would cost me everything I had to possess it.

Who would falter or shrink back at the thought of the price, when the wonder of even being allowed to touch such precious things was being offered? My heart rose up and with all my might I said "yes" to Jesus. Everything in me rejoiced as I stood at this crossroads and in the power of the Spirit had strength to choose the pathway that would lead me further into the depths of God's call upon my life. How I praise Him for always providing us with the strength we need to make the choices that will ultimately fulfil the very desires of our heart.

As the weekend progressed, Claudio shared a personal testimony that plumbed the depths of my world. He spoke about a time in his own life where he had longed for more of God while he was also pastoring a very small church, the green shoots of what would become the mighty 'Rey de Reyes' in Belgrano, Buenos Aires.

Spurred on by this desire for 'more' he visited Benny Hinn's ministry in Florida, in the same way that many from the UK had also to humble themselves and admit that others had something we did not, spending their own money to get on a flight to where God *was* moving. There is something in our taking responsibility to seek and find that which we are looking for that Father notices and approves of. He sets before us the savour of something so good, that we will stir ourselves and reach out for it!

As Claudio spent time in Benny's meetings, he was blessed and Benny even prayed for him personally, although nothing earth-shattering seemed to take place. Returning to his hotel bedroom however, marvelling at the unique way Benny seemed to know the Spirit, Claudio prepared to put the key into his hotel bedroom door and then felt someone push him from behind. Looking around, Claudio was puzzled to see that there was no one there. Quickly stepping in, Claudio was rooted to the spot when he realised that the person who had pushed him was now in the room. Jesus Himself stood before him.

Referring only to the most wonderful surprise, the delight of seeing and being with Jesus, Claudio could share no more of what passed between them as Jesus remained for many hours. It was too holy and too precious to even speak of.

I listened to this testimony as one transfixed. My spirit was attuned to the testimony of this most incredible encounter, as if I was hearing a language spoken for the first time that I was always meant to speak. It is impossible to describe the impact it made and I drank in this truthful account as a man dying of thirst receives a drink of water. The conference ended, I travelled back home carrying the memory of what I'd heard as an entrustment that was so precious to me that I never wanted it to fade.

In the same month, the great Argentine evangelist, Ed Silvoso came to speak in London. Taking a day off work to go and hear him speak, Ed closed his session with an invitation. Lifting up a brochure for his 'International Institute' in Argentina, the annual event which gathered all the forerunning revivalists in that great nation, he set before us the opportunity to be part of another historic gathering and said, "Why don't you ask the Lord to treat you?"

My goodness, how I wanted the Lord to treat me to that trip! I took the brochure home and brooded over it, practically sleeping with it under my pillow. For international delegates the costs were significant enough to rule out my ability to go, outside of a miracle and so I hesitated.

Finally, Kim Cross, a dear Christian brother who is also a businessman, helped push me off the fence as he shared a truth with me, *"The greatest reward always requires the greatest risk Julie. You know something of what you will receive if you go to Argentina, there will be a great reward, but you will have to take the risk first and put all you have into it."* He sowed £500 as the first and most treasured seed into my decision to go.

Two months later, in October 1996, I then travelled with over 50 British people to Buenos Aires for the Harvest Evangelism International Institute led by Ed Silvoso and my life was changed once more. Powerfully impacted by the intensity of the anointing on those Argentine ministers and their people, I witnessed an unprecedented outpouring of the Spirit greater than I'd ever seen, seeing children pray with more power than most adults, receiving vision that a whole city could be won for Christ, learning that because we are seated in Christ in the Heavenly Places we have authority in the those realms to displace entrenched strongholds, it was the most intense corporate spiritual experience of my life.

The potential of the powerful life that we have come into, that is born of the Spirit, was now being set before me as an example of just how effective the Body of Christ can be for the Kingdom's sake. Jesus *is* lifted up and glorified when we corporately move forward to see great breakthroughs personally and at a city-wide level.

One night, half way through the Institute, a great man of God, Carlos Annacondia, preached at a stadium in Mar del Plata. I had heard so much about this man's ministry that the opportunity to hear Annacondia preach was one of the main reasons I had wanted to travel all the way to Argentina in the first place. Moving so powerfully in the anointing of the Spirit that he saw many miracles, personally contributing to whole cities moving into revival, I decided I would go forward for ministry no matter what the appeal was for and so, when his preaching was over he asked for anyone who had a need to come forward. I got straight out of my seat, walked down the flight of stairs and took my place among 2,000 other people.

Everyone was worshipping the Lord. Annacondia came down from the platform and began to pray for the people. I was so far back I knew that he would not be able to pray for me personally but it did not matter, I had come to meet with Jesus and I began to focus all my attention on Him. The worship went on for a long time and this is something I had come to expect because the Argentines worship for hours, not because they just like to take a long time, but because they are *going some-where*. The more we worshipped, the deeper into the presence of God we went and everyone knew it.

After a while, my arms began to tingle and burn. I thought it was because they had been up in the air for too long. Suddenly, the eyes of my spirit were opened and I saw something so wonderful. I saw the Holy Spirit coming towards *me*, with two angels behind him.

He has the most wonderful face, like a person, with radiant golden light emanating from His Being. In the same instant that I saw Him, as He looked at me, the power of the love of God filled me and it was so intense there was no room for anything else at all. The feeling of it was incredible, so powerful that any doubt, any fear, any sense at all that we are not loved by the Father, was gone.

The words are hard to find, it is hard to express what it feels like to be so filled in every part of your being with the love of the Living God, but in that moment the veil between heaven and earth was taken away and I was absolutely touched with the full power of the strength the love of God. The feeling was so intense that I understood why we don't experience it continuously in this life, the power of it is too much for us to contain. Just a few seconds was sufficient to utterly fill my entire being and the memory of it still burns in my heart to this day.

At the same time, I also knew what was on the mind and heart of the Spirit. It is the Spirit that knows the thoughts and mind of God, just as it is our spirit that knows the thoughts of our own mind (1 Corinthians 2:11). In that moment, as the Holy Spirit revealed Himself to me, His thoughts were also revealed to me and I knew that he had come not just for me but for *all* the people. No one was out of his sights. He was full of purpose and authority, moving very fast, it was like he was brooding over us all, flying like an angel does, covering us with His presence, searching out our heart, revealing the presence of Jesus so that we might glorify Him. In the next moment, the experience was over. I was shaken to the core, filled to over-flowing by the power of God's love, my eyes had been opened and now I could see.

The golden thread of the Spirit's ministry, first sewn into my life as a child at Hollybush, then delicately woven through the decades that had followed, culminated in a face-to-face encounter with the Spirit Himself. I knew, with an unshakeable knowing, that God is real. I saw into the realm where the Spirit operates and all that I had read and believed in my heart, that the Spirit is a Person, was gloriously confirmed to me as I saw His wonderful face, as surely as I see my loved ones before me in the natural, that He is real and that He is who Jesus says He is. He is our friend and counsellor, He is the Power of the Lord.

Just as Kathryn Kuhlman experienced extraordinary reactions to her presence when she was nowhere near a church or a meeting because the Spirit attended her, I believe I encountered the Spirit Himself that night because he attended the ministry of Carlos Annacondia and then met personally with *me*.

My longing and my thirst for the deep things of God had taken me all the way to Argentina. My small salary couldn't pay for the costs to go even if I gave two whole month's wages, but just like the boy with the loaves and fishes, or the widow with her last dregs of oil, I know that our Father sees our heart and is moved to perform a miracle, making a way where there seems to be no way. He loves our every attempt to reach out for Him and so with the little that I had, he then multiplied with seeds sown by His people, making the way for me to get there and blessed my life with an encounter so rich, that NO money on earth could ever pay for. I tasted of the sacred realms of Heaven, where the precious and Holy Spirit has His abode, I saw into it for the first time as the veil was lifted from my eyes and such power came into my spirit that it could not be contained.

Months earlier, I had listened to Claudio Freidzon's beautiful account of the night Jesus met personally with him. Immeasurably blessed by this wondrous testimony I would not have dreamed of asking for such a thing for myself and yet the unspoken longing, for such a depth of encounter, was in my heart. My Heavenly Father knew it was there and in His wonderful plan, He drew me to Argentina to immerse me in the sovereign work of the Spirit in that nation and then answer that unspoken cry as I saw the Holy Spirit, face-to-face.

As I write these words, Jesus is reaching out to **you** as the Spirit anoints the truth of what I'm testifying to. In the same way that I longed for the rich experience others had entered into, you are being touched deep in your spirit, to long for the same things too. He sees your heart, he sees your every effort to love and please

Him, He knows the price you've paid and the sacrifices you've made and you too are being called. You are being drawn deeper into the depths of Father's purpose upon your life, as Jesus woos your heart, even this very hour.

AWAKENED HEART

"You shall know the heart of my heart
and this shall be the writing of that, of the Lamb.
You shall write for me, you shall declare, for the
detail is the heart of my heart. Though you are a
daughter, your heart is as John. To the heart is your
ministry. He is placing your ear, there are going to
be times when He is literally going to embrace you
and put you to the heart. That's the days, your days
of knowing, you are called even as John, to know
the heart of the Lamb."

This wonderful prophetic word, given to me by
Johnny Foote at the Houses of Parliament on my return
to England in 2002, sowed seeds of promise that a new
realm of relationship with Jesus was unfolding for me.

How significant that after so many years of blessing,
a face-to-face encounter with the Holy Spirit and many
other rich spiritual experiences, as I began to walk in a
mandate to pray for the destiny of my own nation, I was
now being called into a walk of intimacy with Jesus that
I had never known before. I was to learn that the walk

of intimacy is the key of power that will sustain us through the fiercest of battles.

As much as I already knew about Jesus, the thought of knowing Him so personally made my heart skip a beat. It was very moving and I wondered, perhaps like Mary, how could that be possible, to know Jesus like this? It felt like a deep re-ordering was taking place, from the centre of my being, to learn to live my life and fulfil my calling from a place of total devotion to Him and Him alone.

This prophetic word taught me that even though we may feel we know Jesus well, an invitation will always come from the Spirit to enter into deeper realms still because we can never exhaust the depths of Jesus' love for us, or the extent to which our lives can be transformed by His Presence. We need to press in.

Through this word the Spirit opened my eyes to a greater depth of love and connection with Jesus that I did not even know was possible. I had seen so much and pursued relationship with God with everything in my power for so many years, but I had to learn that there was more to come.

The truth is that Jesus is inviting each one of us to know Him this way, entering into such a reality of relationship with Him that we know the sound of His voice, we recognise when He is near, we begin to believe that He is willing to entrust even His very own heart to us. We are called to pursue Him all the days of our life and those who seek with all of their heart will literally find

God Himself. Every barrier obstructing the way into His Presence, no matter how that barrier became established in the first place, can and will be removed so that we then see Him, face-to-face.

Soon after receiving this prophetic word, I met Liz Jones (now Wright). Liz had been powerfully born-again as she physically met Jesus in an encounter that took place in the Seychelles, in 1995[5] and this profound experience, along with many others that followed, established within Liz a tremendous awareness of her identity as the Bride of Christ. Her life of love and devotion testified to this truth and we became friends instantly.

The overflow of Liz's life in Jesus touched me deeply. The Holy Spirit started to awaken my heart, revealing Jesus to me in a way that was new, causing me to consider my own identity as the Bride of Christ for the very first time.

Who has not read the famous passages in Revelation concerning the marriage supper of the Lamb, the call of the Spirit and the Bride for Jesus to return? But when the Spirit leads us to know *ourselves* as part of the Bride, this astounding truth takes time to absorb, that the One who is utterly perfect sees His Bride in *you* and in *me*...

I followed my heart and discovered that the walk of the Bride begins a profound and challenging journey of

---

[5] Liz Wright's powerful testimony, 'Visitations from Jesus Revealing the Truth and Power of Who We Really Are' is shared in 'Ekklesia Rising', © Liz Wright, 2015, Freedom Publishing

love, where we enter into mature relationship with Jesus, sharing not only His heart, but His thoughts, plans, His very life, knowing what it means to cease our wandering and find rest in Him. The walk of the Bride is an invitation to walk a pathway where, setting everything else aside, even our own desires, we pursue one thing and one alone: relationship with Him.

Line upon line, precept upon precept, as the Spirit led me deeper into this inheritance, the challenges began to come.

Every area of disagreement within, concerning the truth of I am and who He is, had to be removed. Jesus knows the wounds we carry, often hidden and unreached by even years of walking closely with God and He began to bring me close to His side, gently but relentlessly exposing the very experiences that had most damaged my identity, self-worth and hurt my heart.

Deeply held core beliefs surfaced. At times this process was hard as the truth confronted each stronghold, but it is my testimony that the love of Jesus the Bridegroom has the power to heal the wounds that have opposed our ability to rest and be secure in His Love more than any other. The love of the Bridegroom goes right to the very core of who you are like a healing, purifying fire and the enemy of our souls loses his most vital and strategic hold over us as our hearts become free to love Him!

The walk of the Bride is a courageous one, it has extraordinary power to heal because while we may have served Him faithfully, extending His Kingdom each day, for *this* journey with Jesus as your Bridegroom, if you are willing, He will open the door to the deepest recesses of your heart and step in.

There is nothing to fear as every part of who you really are is known. Even now, as you read these words, know that you can entrust your whole heart to the loving hands of your King because He is the One to utterly restore you and cause you to know, *you are His*.

In the years that followed, through many seasons of intercession and strategic assignments in prayer, Liz and I along with our dear friends Lulu and Mary, spent hours in worship and teaching, growing in the knowledge of the truth of the Bride of Christ and her relationship with Jesus as the Bridegroom. Mike Bickle's superlative expositions from the scriptures helped me so greatly, setting in place a foundation of Biblical understanding that is trustworthy for all of God's people.[6]

Inwardly however, I longed for a deeper connection still.

While my brief encounter with the Holy Spirit just a few years before had utterly impacted my life, I had never sought another, always thinking of what happened as a sovereign gift that was rare. As I pursued deep relationship with Jesus however, pressing in,

---

[6] Mike Bickle's extensive and foundational teaching can be found at mikebickle.org

battling in prayer for so many impossible situations, the desire for something more began to grow.

Most of us know what it is to press in for break-throughs in our lives and ministries, sometimes for decades and start to feel that what we know is now insufficient for the circumstances we find ourselves in. The circumstances themselves have been permitted to bring about the need and the desire for growth.

My spirit wrestled with the dissatisfaction I felt at the depth of my own relationship with Jesus while taking comfort in the knowledge that I was being led this way by the Spirit! This lesson I had well and truly learned: that we will always be encouraged to reach out for more and sensing the Spirit's leading I opened up my heart and began honestly to say what I felt, "Jesus, I long to see You..."

Never wanting to demand anything from Him, this process was sometimes like a balancing act: knowing I really needed a new dimension of experience, then releasing this deepest desire to His will and His ultimate right to respond. I could not make anything happen and did not want to. Even today I still believe we cannot and should not try to initiate encounter, that any visitation comes as a sovereign gift of love, but to desire more pleases God and is a key to unlock those new realms of relationship for us.

Edging forward, the Holy Spirit started to show me that the desire to see Jesus, to see God, was in keeping with how we are designed as human beings. As a vital part of our nurture and development our first encounter with love is face-to-face, with parents or loving carers that we daily see. Because of this, while we receive our salvation with the greatest gratitude, treasuring God's Word that daily speaks and feeds us, experiencing the transforming power of the Spirit changing our lives, to desire to see the One who is Love, is normal.

This belief settled in my heart and caused me to keep pressing in.

John the Beloved saw God. He had such a loving relationship with Jesus that the greatest mysteries ever revealed were revealed to *him* and as the circumstances of my life darkened through the early death of my father, the hope that God gave me at such a difficult time was that all the potential of the level of connection that John had is still available to us. In the midst of our greatest pain, we can be sustained by the living and vital connection we have with the Eternal God.

No matter what we walk through in this life, the pressure of our circumstances can be made to serve the purposes of God. Clinging to the promises of God, I pursued His presence even into the valley of the shadow of death, mourning and sad as I was. The knowledge that there is a height of experience, a depth of the knowledge of the glory of the Godhead that we can always reach for, kept me going.

The choices we make at times like these carry tremendous weight. Our simple trust and obedience to faithfully keep going when we aren't sure what we should do, where our surroundings are now dark, unfamiliar and we do not know the way, these are sufficient to order our steps according to the will of God. He is holding us and He is leading us on.

Mourning the loss of my beloved Father, carrying new and pressing family responsibilities that were serious, such were the circumstances I faced. As the Bride, walking a path I would never choose, it seemed that this pathway alone led to the inner door of my heart and Jesus desired to come in. Out of my depth and unable to control my circumstances, daily I relied more and more upon Him.

One winter's morning, many months later, I sat at Liz's kitchen table in the quietness of the dawn, enfolded in the stillness of the peace of the presence of the Lord. Reaching across the table I picked up a sheaf of well-worn papers that caught my eye and began to read what turned out to be an excerpt from France Metcalfe's writings. For many decades, Frances led a very powerful ministry of worship and intercession in Idyllwild, California known as 'The Golden Candlestick',[7] which flowed from her extraordinary walk with Jesus as His Bride.

That morning, I read Frances' own journaling of her very first invitation from Jesus to "Come away" with Him and the incredible face-to-face encounters that

---

[7] The full testimony of Frances Metcalfe and the ministry of 'The Golden Candlestick' is available in Volume 1,2&3 of 'Ladies of Gold' by James Maloney, 'Answering the Cry' Publications

followed. As I read her anointed testimony, the Holy Spirit started to touch my heart very deeply. A thirst and a longing for Jesus seemed to impart from Frances' writing that was so strong I felt Him reach out his hand and invite *me* to "Come Away" with Him too.

A depth of knowledge that I am His Bride manifested in my heart supernaturally as I leaned into this sovereign invitation and said, "Yes. Wherever You desire to take me, I will come away with You. You are all I long for." For days I could not pull out of this experience, such that no matter what I was doing or who I was with, Jesus was all I could think about.

Seasons of faithfulness and obedience will always cause us to grow and bear fruit but that morning, through the on-going power of a truthful testimony, Jesus Himself reached out to me from eternity and there was a release of the knowledge of the truth into my spirit. I supernaturally crossed a threshold from faith to the experiential knowledge of Jesus the Bridegroom as the reality of His love and desire to be with me reached the very depths of my heart. His love connected with mine and I felt it. A healing took place sufficient for a new and tangible foundation to settle in my heart and from that day, the walk of intimacy began to unfold as the Prophet foretold.

Perhaps there is always the need for Jesus Himself to call each one of us as His Bride, for a supernatural intervention where we personally experience His invitation and even though for me, this came just one quiet morning as I simply read from Frances Metcalfe's journals, it was enough to effect deep and lasting change.

Expectantly I began now to turn my heart towards Jesus on a much deeper level, empowered in a new way to love Him, knowing it is the highest calling of my life to return the love that He has for me. Circumstances change, good times and difficult times will come and go, there will be fruit in our lives and ministry, but to stead-fastly love Him and grow in relationship with Him is the most important priority of our lives. As the Bride, to this calling we will always return.

My prayer is that you too will experience a sover-eign, personal invitation, in an unmistakeable and life-changing way, as the Spirit leads you into new realms of the love of Jesus. If there is desire in your heart to know Him more deeply, then your Heavenly Father will never fail to satisfy that desire with the very best of good things: His Precious Son.

Within weeks Jesus started to impress upon my heart that because of my call to the nation, I would walk out my own relationship with Him as His Bride knowing that with every victory, where my heart turned ever more towards Him, this process of inner transformation would speak of the nation's turning back to Him.

When God calls you to pray for a nation, where you stand personally will greatly impact the effectiveness of those prayers. To the measure we are surrendered to the transforming work of the Spirit in our lives, we are being uniquely prepared and positioned with authority, for great effectiveness in the battles being fought in the heavenly realm over the country in which we live.

For a nation like England, rich in strength and natural ability, acknowledging God or the need for Divine assistance does not come naturally or easily and yet this does not change the fact that without Him, we will not achieve one fraction of His true purpose.

Through the Bride in England's increasing willingness to completely depend upon Jesus, filled with the truth of *our* ascended position, seated in Him, loving Him, humbly depending on Him for everything, authority sufficient to start to dismantle even the most deeply entrenched, prideful, national stronghold is generated. We then begin to pull the nation into the correct alignment before God, one prayer, one assignment at a time.

How significant that the walk of intimacy with Jesus generates the kind of authority that we need to rule, from Heaven's perspective, concerning a nation's standing before God!

We have power to affect the affairs of a nation the more we are hidden in Him. Transcending the circumstances of the natural realm, we walk a powerful journey of love as the Royal Bride, loving Jesus for who He is, being known by Him, satisfying His heart with the love of ours. As the sceptre rests in our hands, we release power as we yield to His love and align ourselves with the truth of who we are and who He is. Even the nations of the earth can be healed by the powerful intercession of the Bride of Christ, each one made ready and presented in all their glory to the Bridegroom, whose inheritance they are.

In the springtime of 2012 Liz was married to Wesley Wright and as they took their vows, glimpses of the promise of our future union with Jesus shone through. For me, it felt like their marriage was a prophetic sign, that the Body and Bride of Christ is entering into a new era where, within our natural union as men and women, the glory of God will be revealed so powerfully that everyone will be able to see it.

Brimming over with the joy of such a holy, significant occasion, as Maid of Honour I received Liz's bouquet. The next day I packed the car for our family's return home and as I held the bouquet in my hands for a moment, the atmosphere became very still, thick and heavy.

Suddenly, Jesus Himself stood at my right side. I saw Him with the eyes of my spirit, just as vividly as if He was physically standing there. There was an intense, glorious fragrance around Him and I sensed His great kindness, His gentle heart, saw only His hands as they reached out, took the bouquet of white roses from me and placed it into my heart. I saw the bouquet pass through my very being and then He said, "This is My promise to you."

In those sacred moments, Jesus showed *me* in the most beautiful and moving way the unfailing, steadfast covenant of His love. He placed His promise of eternal commitment in my heart. I started to hear a multitude, precious members of His Body crying out, as though they were perishing for lack of vision because they could not see or experience that which their own hearts were longing to know. Oh, how deeply they needed the same certainty of committed, eternal love that goes beyond faith to become an experiential, living foundation in their own life... Then Jesus said, "Tell My People. I desire the truth to be established in their hearts. Tell my people the truth so that they can LIVE."

As the sweetness of His presence ebbed away, my first encounter with Jesus came to an end. I felt the justice of God power into my spirit, that where the enemy had robbed my family line in so many ways, Father was now raising me up to experience and release the truth of who we are as the Bride, because it is His desire to establish the same covenant promise in the hearts of every one of His Beloved Children, in a manner that cannot be shaken.

There is so much more for you to enter into as Jesus now reaches out his hand to *you*, inviting you to "Come Away" with Him. His promise of Love is sure. Nothing can stand in the way of His faithful, covenant commitment to bring you forth as His chosen Bride, without spot or wrinkle, pure, holy and powerful.

There is a pathway set before you. It will lead to your heart and will awaken your heart to the great love of *your* King.

THE MANTLE OF PURITY

Moving with intensity now, just a few weeks later the Spirit led me to the One He loves and in the midst of a time of corporate worship, I received the deepest desire of my heart as Jesus came and knelt in front of me.

His beauty is impossible to describe. He had a heavy golden crown upon His head, resting on dark shoulder-length hair, then for a moment, with just one unforgettable glance, he looked into my eyes and placed a heavy mantle around my shoulders. It was a Mantle of Purity. Silver coloured, about an inch thick and tying at my neck, it reached all the way to the floor.

The purity was Jesus' own and it began to infuse my whole being, filling and touching every part of me like a cleansing, glorious river, so powerful I felt it breaking the hold of any residue of defilement from my life's journey. The scars and bruises on my heart came under the healing power of this most personal touch from the King and I was deeply connected to Jesus in the very depths of my being. Such complete fulfilment was released into my life that I tasted the very goodness of

God and was satisfied. From that moment on, there was absolutely no desire to seek fulfilment from any other source because all of my needs were met, in Him.

In those incredible and precious moments, David's exhortation to *'Worship the Lord in the Beauty of Holiness'* Psalm 29:2 became very real. As the Mantle was laid upon me, the liberty I felt revealed a powerful truth, that Holiness, which is *'to be chaste and innocent of sin'* is beautiful because it is full of joy, liberty and LIFE.

This encounter showed me that holiness is the fruit of being connected to the purity of Jesus Himself as we abide in Him. Holiness is nothing to do with a straight-jacket of restriction or religious disciplines of self-control, where we try in our own strength to lead a life we hope will be found acceptable to Him. We are already acceptable to Him, we are fully accepted in the Beloved and while there is a need to walk wisely and honour the guidelines set before us in Scripture, apart from this there is nothing more we can do to perfect ourselves. As I worshipped Jesus that day, little by little learning how to absorb myself in His Presence and rest, He then appeared before me as the King to prepare me more deeply now, as His Bride.

Unaware of my own need or what was possible for my life, Jesus chose the timing to lay His mantle upon me. The sovereign gift of His own virtue instantly provided supernatural power to live a holy life and the freedom of it cascaded throughout my entire being. Never, in all of my life had I felt like that. The reality of who Jesus is and what He has done in redeeming our lives was made known to me on a brand-new level and as my heart exploded with joy, I worshipped Him in a way that I knew was beautiful *to Him*.

It is truly possible to become so completely free that we walk in holiness and nothing mars the beauty of the way we worship Jesus and through Him, the Father. This is how the Word is incarnated in our lives. I moved from knowing the scripture that we are to 'worship the Lord in the beauty of holiness', to being supernaturally filled with holiness so that I could worship Jesus in a way that is beautiful. Once you have tasted the depths of the goodness of God like this, a holy appetite springs to your tongue so that you desire more and more of Him!

Jesus gave me this precious mantle for my own life but I knew it was also a sign of His desire to release His own purity to **all** of His people.

It is His desire for *you* to experience the power and freedom His purity offers, as a gift of love. We can never become pure at this level by our own efforts and Jesus wants us to know His heart's desire, that through Him and only Him we will be brought into a state of holiness, no matter what we have been through.

As Jesus knelt before me that day and released this part of His strength into my life, I also saw and touched a place in Him of total restoration, experiencing all the perfection of Jesus Himself, His ability to heal and redeem our gender and even our sexuality. His Bride will come forth without spot, wrinkle or blemish as Jesus Himself provides this transforming power.

The key of access to all that He is, is His love for us. As we love Him in return, surrendering to His ways and His rule in our life as our Lord and King, we can begin to experience for ourselves the truth that:

"In Him we live and move and have our being" Acts 17:28

All that He is can become ours as we let go of our attempts to live life well before Him and learn to literally live our lives inside of Christ Himself. At rest in Him, He can then begin to pour into us all that we need, direct from His own source of supply.

And so, as I worshipped Jesus that summer day among a small group of devoted believers at Beacon House of Prayer in Stoke on Trent, He sovereignly revealed Himself to me, face-to-face, completely filling me with a grace that came direct from His very own Person and I was changed. **I became like Him.**

Jesus knows that we not only need His purity to walk in holiness, but that we need the protection it offers. In times like these there is more pressure than ever before, bringing temptation and the opportunity to compromise into our lives. Daily we are bombarded with sights and sounds that defile us and through lack of power to live a holy life, the bar wavers to the extent that the Body of Christ is no longer certain how much freedom we can expect to have. We may even wonder what holiness is.

The truth for this hour is that Jesus is raising that bar to its ultimate level as He releases His purity into our lives to the extent that we are not only free but we can ascend and rule over all the defilement that the enemy sends against us!

Jesus is preparing a spotless Bride so full of power and victory that the testimony of our lives, as we come forth in His holiness, will offer tremendous hope to a broken world because the glory of God is literally being revealed in us. His holiness for our un-holiness. His Beauty for our ashes. We will shine so clearly and with such power that people will be drawn to the brightness of the light of Jesus in us, hungry for the abundant life He offers and link by link, the chains of their bondage will be broken.

Walking in this level of revelation, shining with His light, we will powerfully demonstrate the truth that it is possible for men and women as the pinnacle of the Creation, not only to walk in Holiness as a sign and a wonder, but to walk in the glory and the pristine purity of manhood and womanhood, as God originally intended.

The enemy has sought to afflict us with multiple wounds in the most fundamental and personal areas of life, but Jesus has already overcome in this battle and He has a victory for us that will testify of His goodness, to the whole world. We were made for abundant life, filled with the liberty and fulfilment that holiness provides and it is His intention to make sure we receive it.

And so, it can be no mistake that the Mantle of Purity was inches thick, covering me all the way down to my feet. Its leaves of silver protected me as surely as a suit of armour. Nothing, no flaming arrow of the evil one who seeks to defile and destroy, can get through! This kind of purity equips you for victory in the fiercest of battles; we need it, it is powerful and it is only available IN Him.

From the day that I saw Him there is now an inexhaustible, indwelling flow of purity that comes from Jesus Himself as I rest and abide in Him. This flow of provision has protected and empowered me to live an abundant life, totally free from the rule of the carnal nature and I live with a constant sense of the incredible victory this represents.

This does not mean that I judge others according to the level of freedom Jesus has given to me, or that I shrink away from the reality of how many live their lives, the opposite is actually true. Jesus' heart on this subject has been made known to me. I feel His tremendous love and concern for all people, for the robbery of so much innocence, for the pain and brokenness people are forced to live with, knowing deep in my spirit that something so precious has been stolen from that man or woman, that girl or boy, even from the Body and Bride of Christ and Jesus wants to give it back!

THE PROVERBS 31 WIFE

In the winter of 2012, a few months after this powerful encounter with Jesus, Liz and I were in a time of intercession as our ministry, 'The Bridal Company', was being established. In the spirit, I saw the Proverbs 31 wife come and stand at the kitchen table where we were seated.

Spotlessly clean and dressed in immaculate linen, the Proverbs 31 wife came with her sleeves rolled up in readiness for work. Though silent, her steady brown eyes conveyed something to me: that she had come as a sign, pointing the way to important truths that could be gleaned from her example. The glory of her shining, yet practical appearance portrayed an excellence in our earthly labours, as worship before God, that was inspirational. Her visit caused me to go straight to the scriptures to read Proverbs 31.

What a vivid and compelling account of the relationship she had with her husband, who sat confidently in the gate of the city. As I read of the masterful way she worked, ran her household, looked after her children,

took care of the poor, bought land and made invest-
ments, all these things spoke deeply into my heart.

Who has not read her story and been impressed by
her accomplishments or inspired by the stability of this
family and the contribution they made to the society
they lived in? It was overwhelming to realise that Jesus
was speaking to me of His desire that *we* are to be just
as fruitful, that He believes we are just as capable of
achieving the same level of nurture and fulfilment that
the Proverbs 31 household enjoyed. The question I had
to ask was, how?

In each one of us there is a deep-seated desire not just
to know what is possible but to *see* the transforming
power of God manifest in the heart of our personal
lives, our family and our homes. In this hour, I believe
this to be one of the most crucial battles of all and we
will have to contend for the victory. We need vision and
we need to know *how* to contend that we may see the
full manifestation of God's purpose for marriage and
family, right in the heart of our homes.

Perceiving the strategic and purposeful nature of
the visit of the Proverbs 31 wife, I began to study the
passage in scripture more deeply, looking for keys of
wisdom that this couple knew, keys producing such outstanding fruit that their example was lifted up and per-
manently honoured in the Word of God.

There is a lot we can learn from the rich account of
this woman's conduct and her inspiring work ethic, but
in Proverbs 31: 11 my attention was drawn to a

fascinating dynamic in her marriage: the husband had entrusted his heart to his wife:

"The heart of her husband trusts in her [with secure confidence] and he will have no lack of gain."

The Proverbs 31 wife was such a trustworthy woman that her husband had confidence to lay bare the most precious part of himself, his heart, and as a result, she knew who he really was. Night and day, she carried his deepest desires, his very destiny and as she did so, *he* had no lack of gain. The surrounding protection and empowerment she provided for her husband was the Divinely appointed, supernatural key to his success. What an amazing insight. What a jewel of wisdom for us, as relevant now as it was in their day.

For this couple, as he made himself totally vulnerable to his wife we then see him securely established in the seat of power, the Governmental gate. Biblical 'city gates' were the place of government where all the important decisions were made and it is interesting to see that as a result of the trust and intimacy between them, he was seated, peacefully exercising a Governmental role. No striving or vying to be there. The intimate bond between them gave him a powerful source of Godly strength that enabled him to occupy his rightful place. Their union influenced and helped uphold the government of the whole city!

The fruit of the trustworthy stewardship of his heart was that *her* work was known and praised in the very same gate of influence too. If he had not been able to give his whole heart to his wife, one can only wonder how securely he would have been established in the Governmental gate, or whether her name would ever have been mentioned there at all.

It may appear that all men are not called, as the Proverbs 31 husband was called, to a literal Governmental gate, but there is a truth for us to access from their story. The Kingdom of God is within us. We all have a mandate to manifest the Kingdom on earth as it is in Heaven and this means that we will bring the Government of Heaven to bear, in the spheres of influence God has appointed for us.

Every man is therefore called to exercise the Government of the Kingdom, wherever he is called to serve, using the gifts God gave him. I believe we are being shown that where, in the marriage alignment, the wife receives the sacred entrustment of her husband's heart, this is a vital key to seeing that man established in the governmental position of his own Kingdom mandate, whatever this may be. Without her, the supernatural empowerment he needs will not be available to undergird or ensure his efforts.

Could it be possible that this one truth alone is sufficient for marriages to be consistently under attack?

It was moving to realise that Jesus is showing us that *a man's ability to fully achieve his God-given destiny lies in the trustworthy hands of his wife.* Whether married or presently single, as this revelation dawns on us we can see that women are being offered a breath-taking responsibility: to be found trustworthy in the life-long stewardship of a husband's heart. In return, the men are being drawn by the Spirit to be willing to trust, to lean in to the surrounding strength of their wives and share the very deepest essence of who they are. Something mystical and very wonderful starts to happen as together, they then plumb the depths of God's call upon their marriage.

I believe the visit of the Proverbs 31 wife was intended first of all, to highlight the beauty and power of such synergy, a fulfilment that went beyond this couple being in love and establishing a good home for their children.

Skilful as she was, her greatest accomplishment had to have been the way she carried her husband's heart because the scriptures show us that he truly lacked for nothing. As husband and father, he was safe in the love of his wife, exercising his governmental role, enjoying abundant provision and their whole family was then securely established as the Proverbs 31 passage so richly describes. This, I believe, is the wisdom the Spirit is showing us: that the blessing they enjoyed and for which they have been celebrated for thousands of years, flowed from the incredible, God-given intimacy of their connection. We are being inspired to believe for the same, whether we have been married for years or are still believing to be so.

What comes first? To trust someone, or, for that someone to first demonstrate that they are worthy to be trusted? As the revelation from the Proverbs 31 marriage flowed, it seems that the greater responsibility here, and from which example we are supposed to learn, is on the woman. Her faithful spirit enabled her to create an authentic environment of safety and loyalty, giving her husband good reason to make himself vulnerable and share his heart with her. We now have the vantage point from the Spirit to see and understand what the scripture is telling us: that so much blessing hangs upon his ability to do so: *"The heart of her husband trusts in her [with secure confidence], And he will have no lack of gain."*

The visit of the Proverbs 31 wife caused me to contemplate the hidden power of trust, how powerful it is when we are trustworthy in thought, word and deed. It instilled an awareness to prioritise that which God so clearly values. As the battle over marriage rages, we as women can press in to the presence of God to understand the greater prize being set before us, seeking the grace and ability to loyally steward the revelation of the essence of who God has made our husbands to be and never betray that trust. Many attractions draw a couple together, but it is the trustworthiness of the woman that unlocks the depths of that which God has placed in a man's heart. Pure poetry.

The more I dwelled on the story of this outstanding couple, the secret of the renowned financial success of the Proverbs 31 wife then became clear as I saw that their union is also an allegory[8] speaking of the union between Jesus and His Bride.

---

[8] An allegory is a story in which people, things and happenings have a hidden or symbolic meaning.

Ephesians 5:23 tells us, "*For the husband is the head of the wife as also Christ is the Head of the Church.*" Colossians 2:19 goes on to then share a powerful truth concerning our ability to increase, "*Holding fast to the Head, from whom all the body, nourished and knit together by joints and ligaments, grows with the increase that is from God.*" From this we see that it is **only** as we are connected to the Head that we are nourished and grow with the increase that comes from God because He is the source of all the growth and all the provision that we need. That connection is so important that we need to spend time meditating on its meaning, absorbing the truth until we are inwardly and deeply connected to Jesus, personally experiencing the provision and growth that can only come from Him.

As a type of the Bride (the Church/Ekklesia) the Proverbs 31 wife is so prosperous because her husband, as a type of the Bridegroom, is loving his wife as Jesus loves His Bride and doing it so well that she has been able to align herself to him. A manifold flow of blessing and provision that benefits everyone in the family is being released into the marriage as they prophetically walk out between them the alignment between Jesus as the Source, and His Body, His Bride.

It is inspiring to see that as this couple mirrored the union of Jesus and His Bride, her ability to recognise who her husband was and honour him did not diminish her own significance, it positioned her for a life of remarkable meaning. While she undoubtedly worked extremely hard, there was a supernatural wind of the spirit propelling her every effort as she carried her husband's heart in the secret place before God. She accessed the limitless resources that can only be found in Him and one of the most powerful anointings for business that the Scriptures ever recorded was released to her.

The implications of this prophetic truth are that when a married couple reflect this same powerful and prophetic alignment in *their* marriage, they too can tap into a blueprint for provision as they are supernaturally positioned to flourish and prosper in a manner that we have been crying out for.

Proverbs 31 also powerfully turns on its head any assumption that only the husband can or should provide as we consider the husband seated in the Governmental gate, ruling over the affairs of the city, enjoying the financial stability that has come into the family as a result of his *wife's* skilful business dealings. The family was enabled to prosper because their marriage showcased the Headship of Jesus the Source of our supply, the Bride cleaving to Him and the rich provision of Heaven being released. The same supernatural alignment for prosperity is available to us, whether one person is the breadwinner or both.

The Proverbs 31 wife came as I was seated at Liz's kitchen table, just a few months after Jesus had given me the Mantle of Purity. While my heart and spirit were still bathed in the glory of Jesus' gift to me, the wife most famed for her excellence and industry briefly appeared in what we all consider to be the heart of the home.

I love the fact that as I had been daily enjoying His presence, through this encounter and the deep study of scripture that followed, Jesus also drew my attention to the work of our hands, how His Bride can achieve the same excellence and effectiveness that the Proverbs 31 wife enjoyed.   He is interested in our fruitfulness and desires that we bear fruit in abundance.

The Proverbs 31 family prospered as she and her husband were united in a lifetime covenant of intimacy and trust. Their story underlined an essential truth that as we walk in intimacy with Jesus, we will achieve our greatest level of productivity, no matter what we are called to do. The work of our hands is intended to glorify Him.

As we personally take up our position of rest, acknowledging His Headship, abiding in Him, we will receive from Him a powerful flow of provision, of creativity and anointing that no money on earth can buy and it will establish and multiply everything we set our hands to. The quality and savour of the fruit that we will produce will indeed remain, bringing glory to His Name.

In this season of increased understanding, the prophetic word I received, that I would "know the heart of the Lamb like John" now took on even greater meaning. The depth of revelation John the Beloved received was so profound that God's people are still studying the intricate, myriad details of the realm of Heaven, the Government of God and the unfolding of our own future that he wrote about. It is clear that Jesus trusted John completely and that is why He poured out the very secrets of Heaven into this man's life.

As the trustworthy Bride of Christ, growing in stature and proving our faithfulness to Jesus through our joys and sorrows, triumphs and failures, we too will receive revelation of the deepest recesses of His heart as Jesus leans into us. We are being drawn, to enter into faithful stewardship of the very thoughts, dreams and desires of the King...

THE QUEEN OF HEAVEN

When Jesus called me as His Bride, He gave me a new level of revelation of His heart for men, women and for marriage and I gladly received the hope and encouragement He brought. Many of us know that we have often battled in these areas, sometimes for decades, so that many even within the Body of Christ have been left with just fragments of hope for blessing and fruitfulness in their personal lives, marriages and on the home front.

Why have we suffered so relentlessly in this way? And for our children, what will they face as the building blocks of family life are being eroded before our very eyes?

The truth is that we are specifically being warred against and it is the heart of God that we would have wisdom and understanding in these matters, discerning the nature of the spiritual powers opposing us, that we may:

> *"Keep Satan from taking advantage of us,*
> *for we are not ignorant of his schemes."*
> 2 Corinthians 2:11

In May 2014 the season for specific discernment concerning *who* is opposing us in these arenas unfolded for me, as dear friends introduced me to a wonderful, born-again Franciscan Friar. What a divine appointment this turned out to be as this humble man of God shared with me about the mandate of the Queen of Heaven, a high-ranking spiritual power whose works had become well known to him through her many manifestations within churches who allowed the worship of Mary.

Years before, during my time with Ed Silvoso and the Harvest Evangelism team, we often ministered in Argentina and I would hear references to this spirit by local ministers and intercessors, but then and in all the years that followed, despite much experience and insight gleaned concerning spiritual warfare, the Holy Spirit kept this subject closed for me personally, until now.

With the quiet authority of someone who had personally faced this battle for decades, my Catholic friend offered crucial insights as he talked about the personality of this spiritual power operating in the heavenly places:

- The mandate of the Queen of Heaven is to usurp the Headship of Jesus and rule in His place
- She will never submit to His Lordship
- The Queen of Heaven is a more powerful and devastating spirit than Jezebel
- Jezebel works for her
- Where Jezebel can manifest as a false Prophetess, Queen of Heaven manifests as false Apostolic
- If she cannot kill an Apostolic work she will try to take it over and establish a counterfeit

- Wherever there is a strong manifestation of the Queen of Heaven, the Gospel is suppressed as a result

These are sobering insights, each one worthy of much prayer and consideration.

After years of prayer and intercession for many Kingdom initiatives, my spirit witnessed to the truth of what I was hearing because I recognised the fruit of her mandates. For years I had puzzled over significant Christian initiatives relentlessly battling to retain the power of the Spirit in which they were birthed or, changing so gradually, that one did not notice anything amiss until years had passed and it became clear that the original vision no longer lived. The question that I, and many others had been asking was, why?

Turning to scripture to look for references to this high-ranking spirit, I found that Jeremiah chapters 7 and 44 records the idolatry of the Jews exiled in Egypt and their refusal to turn away from the worship of the Queen of Heaven:

"18 The children gather wood, the fathers kindle the fire, and the women knead the dough to make cakes for the queen of heaven; and they pour out drink offerings to other gods that they may offend and provoke Me to anger." Jeremiah 7:18

15 Then all the men who knew that their wives were burning sacrifices to other gods, and all the women who were standing by, a large group, including all the

people who were living in Pathros in the land of Egypt, answered Jeremiah, saying, [16] *"As for the word (message) that you have spoken to us in the name of the Lord, we are not going to listen to you.* [17] *But rather we will certainly perform every word of the vows we have made: to burn sacrifices to the queen of heaven (Ishtar) and to pour out drink offerings to her, just as we ourselves and our forefathers, our kings and our princes did in the cities of Judah and in the streets of Jerusalem; for [then] we had plenty of food and were prosperous and saw no misfortune.* [18] *But since we stopped burning sacrifices to the queen of heaven and pouring out drink offerings to her, we have lacked everything and have been consumed by the sword and by famine."* [19] *And said the wives, "When we were burning sacrifices to the queen of heaven and were pouring out drink offerings to her, was it without [the knowledge and approval of] our husbands that we made cakes [in the shape of a star] to represent her and pour out drink offerings to her?"*
Jeremiah 44:15-20

'Online Bible Gateway' comments as follows on these passages: "A goddess of fertility, probably the Babylonian title for Ishtar. She is identified with the planet Venus. Offerings to this goddess included cakes made in the shape of a star (44:19)."[9]

Also, "Concerning this heathen goddess, Assyrian cult practices invaded God's own precincts and by

---

[9] On-Line Bible Gateway Footnotes: Jeremiah 7:18

Jeremiah's time became a flood. Even within the temple area the worship of heavenly bodies—sun, moon, planets and constellations—had been established. Ishtar, the planet Venus, appeared as the queen of heaven, who as morning star was goddess of war and as evening star was goddess of love and harlotry. This supposed queen was worshiped on the housetops of the city and the whole family in every household was employed in the ritual of her worship—children would gather fuel, fathers would kindle the fires, and the women would knead the dough and make cakes to her honor."[10]

Pondering over this important information, I knew that the Holy Spirit was giving us a vantage point, lifting us up over a battle that has been raging for thousands of years, a battle that beset the children of Israel themselves.

As significant as this spirit appears to be, I found assurance in the knowledge that such understanding was being released only at the time when the clarion call is sounding louder than ever, calling us to personally and corporately pursue Jesus as our life's highest calling. The battle is real but we are not called to battle with spiritual powers. Only He has the virtue and power that we need to not only withstand the influence of such spirits, but to see their centuries-long influence stamped out.

---

[10] On-Line Bible Gateway Resources: All the Women of the Bible>Chapter44> Symbolic & Representative Bible Women> Queen of Heaven

Our pursuit of relationship with Jesus brings great personal blessing into our lives and Scripture also tells us we are seated with Him, in the heavenly places, as a testimony of the manifold wisdom of God. To whom?

"The purpose is that through the church (Ekklesia) the complicated, many-sided wisdom of God in all its infinite variety and innumerable aspects might now be made known to the angelic rulers and authorities (principalities and powers) in the heavenly sphere." Ephesians 3: 10

In Jesus, as His Body, we have therefore been *strategically* positioned to overcome in a battle that is being fought in the heavenlies.[11]

The wisdom I have learned in intercession, through years of experience, is that the more we become like Jesus, manifesting the wisdom of God in and through our lives, the more authority we have to effectively testify of this wisdom in the heavenly realms, standing in the opposite spirit to all that comes against us from the enemy's kingdom.[12] This is *how* we maintain our position as the Body, under Jesus as the Head, whose feet are victoriously established in the lowest realms of hell itself.

---

[11] The original revelation of the strategic nature of this Biblical truth became known to me as I read Ed Silvoso's groundbreaking book 'That None Should Perish', © 1994, Ed Silvoso, Regal Books

[12] The principle of Authority as we come in the 'opposite spirit' was first shared with me in 2000 by Arthur Burke, Sapphire Leadership Group

We are not called to war or fight against any spirit, but when we are able to say of the enemy, like Jesus, *"He has no claim on Me [no power over Me nor anything that he can use against Me];"* John 14:30, every battle we face from the spiritual realm can be won.

It is only as the enemy finds something of his *own nature* in us that our effective position in the heavenlies is weakened and he is then able to use that weakness against us. The more we are filled with the virtue of Jesus' character and nature, such footholds and anchors are dismantled.

This is a very powerful weapon! Powerful enough to ultimately repel the influence of every spirit, lifting us up and over the enemy's every assignment.

Little by little as we become more like Jesus, we are not only transformed, we incrementally earn the authority to maintain our position in the heavenly realm, standing against the enemy's hierarchy, being positioned to rule over it as our lives resoundingly testify of the manifold wisdom of God throughout the heavens, as is our blood-bought destiny.

Knowing therefore from the Scriptures, that the Queen of Heaven has maintained a position of high level influence for centuries, I began to pray, waiting on the Holy Spirit, to discern specifically the authority we need *to come in the opposite spirit*, that we may resist her influence and agenda.

Asking one of my Catholic friend's intercessors what the Lord had shown them, she responded, *"Concerning intercession around the Queen of Heaven, I have always sensed that the opposite of this entity is apparent in the Proverbs 31 woman."*

I was impacted. Very few people were aware of the encounter I'd had with the Proverbs 31 wife nearly two years earlier, or the conviction I held that the beauty and power of the union of Jesus and His Bride is prophetically being revealed in her marriage.

As I 'joined the dots' my spirit witnessed to this amazing suggestion, seeing that the dynamic between the Proverbs 31 wife and her husband would indeed come in the opposite spirit to the queen of heaven, whose agenda is to usurp the Headship of Christ. The Proverbs 31 wife was everything the queen of heaven is not: able to honour and promote the head, who was her husband.

This insight provided confirmation that Jesus was leading me in this unfolding journey of specific revelation and while the influence of the Queen of Heaven is pervasive, as we will see, He showed me that there is much that we are able to do to retrieve the ground she has historically been able to hold.

Knowing that a major part of her assignment is to usurp the Headship of Jesus and rule in His place, as individuals we powerfully come in the *opposite spirit* to her as we daily align ourselves under the security and authority of Jesus' Headship.

Our personal freedom from the rebellion she celebrates generates an *earned authority sufficient to displace her influence from our lives and sphere of influence.* Therefore, while it is our rightful place to be aligned to the Headship of Jesus, this is also a powerful *strategic* position that we cannot afford to give away.

Every married couple in Christ, as they mirror the union and alignment of Jesus and His Bride, has the unique ability to generate authority and become, as one, a weapon powerful enough to oppose this spirit's mandate.

The more we cleave to Jesus as the Head, personally and in our marriages, the more powerful we will become. *This spirit cannot operate in our presence because there is no trace of the mandate she carries within us.*

Imagine the increasing liberty we will experience as this revelation settles in our spirits and we begin to exercise the authority we have, simply by living under Jesus' Headship as the Word exhorts us to do!

One day, following this revelation, I had a vision where Jesus then began to show me the Queen of Heaven's assault on the Apostolic ministry, revealing to me her warfare against the institution of marriage itself.

What does the Apostolic have to do with marriage? In the vision, the Holy Spirit showed me that when a man and a woman become one, they have the ability to procreate and the purpose and calling on this child existed in Heaven first:

"For You formed my innermost parts; You knit me (together) in my mother's womb. I will give thanks and praise to You, for I am fearfully and wonderfully made; Wonderful are Your works, and my soul knows it very well. My frame was not hidden from You, When I was being formed in secret, and intricately and skilfully formed (as if embroidered with many colours) in the depths of the earth, your eyes have seen my unformed substance; And in Your book were all written the days that were appointed for me, when as yet there was not one of them (even taking shape)" Psalm 139: 13-16

"Then the word of the Lord came to me, saying: "Before I formed you in the womb I knew you: Before you were born I sanctified you; I ordained you a prophet to the nations." Jeremiah 1:4-6

I was shown that, as procreation releases into the earth realm that which first existed in Heaven, **this is an apostolic work** and it is just the beginning, an indication of that which a couple can birth between them.

So many couples have not realised the power of who they are as ONE and what they have the ability to achieve together.

A married couple in this kind of union has an apostolic ability to take hold of heavenly blueprints, establishing them in the earth realm and it is for this reason that the Queen of Heaven would absolutely target, undermine and attempt to destroy the marriage of any couple and *especially one between two anointed people.*

No wonder Christian marriages have been under such attack, where, as this spirit is able to successfully divide a married couple, the apostolic union and the work thereof is brought to an end. Not being able to marry is also just as devastating and deathly an outcome as having a marriage destroyed.

Remembering from the initial insights that the Queen of Heaven will set herself up as a counterfeit, in the area of our lives that is most holy, our sexuality, her agenda deepens further as she lures us to open a door and invite her into our lives as a counterfeit partner, encouraging us to seek sexual fulfilment for ourselves, without a husband or wife or in-spite of them.

Natasha Vermaak in her handbook 'Repentance' taught several years ago that our participation in masturbation or pornography is not neutral, that any emission from our body is prized by the spirit realm and goes to an altar which is in the spirit.[13]   The sobering implications for us are therefore, that while no other person may be there with us, such activity is spiritually loaded.

If we can be persuaded to step out of God's design for sexual fulfilment, which is for a married couple in their apostolic calling, to be covered by the Glory of God in the holiness of physical union, then as we seek fulfilment on our own, whether married or single, we are inviting a very subtle counterfeit partner into our lives who is taking the place of a God-given spouse.

As we do so, we are becoming ensnared in an agreement with the Queen of Heaven when we don't even know it.

---

[13] Ariel Gate Africa Publications (PTY) Ltd, 2009, P96-99, P102, 109, 110

Counterfeit works have been established elsewhere in our culture, in plain sight. Freemasonry, a secretive network of men in the marketplace now reaching around the entire globe, is nothing less than a counterfeit apostolic work over which the Queen of Heaven, as the ruling female deity, presides. What an insight for us, as we consider effective ways in which to bring the Kingdom of God into the global marketplace where *another* kingdom has already infiltrated and established itself.

This reality is no longer hidden in the dark, it has been brought into the light so that we can see and keys of wisdom are being placed in our hands to help us overturn the enemy's strategy.

Knowing that we overcome as we walk in the opposite spirit, as marketplace ministers we can see the vital necessity to daily surrender and align under the Headship of Jesus. As we do, we will then step into the ultimate position for effective ministry in the marketplace, displacing the Queen of Heaven by our surrender to His Headship. The more the Body does so, the more corporate authority we have.

It is so interesting to see that Ed Silvoso has championed for many years the central importance of strong marriages and families, as the centrepiece and foundation of the transformation message he is carrying. Ed feels the key to breakthrough as we work to 'disciple a nation' is to see the Kingdom of God being brought into the marketplace and now we have seen that the Queen of Heaven has been firmly established in the heavenlies over the global marketplace, as she presides over the Masonic structure currently operating there.

It is obvious that the Holy Spirit has led Ed in great wisdom to honour and promote the institution of marriage generally and within the Transformation message, because we now know that *strong marriages aligned in Christ are a huge key to displacing the Queen of Heaven*, in the marketplace and wherever she is manifested.

Her work to undermine the presence of the apostolic ministry in the marketplace can be displaced by two powerful weapons: our alignment with Jesus as the Head and by the apostolic anointing flowing from a marriage that is deeply established in Him.

The ultimate mandate of the Queen of Heaven however is to challenge the headship of Jesus Himself, the implication being that her aim is to make herself the head.

We can see this influence in churches where Mary is elevated over Jesus to the extent that she becomes more important than Him and more of a focus. Under such a spiritual climate, the Gospel is hard to preach.

As the Queen of Heaven pursues her agenda to usurp the Headship of Jesus and rule in His place, her warfare intensifies against the Body of Christ, the Bride, ultimately to get us to *turn away from Jesus as our Head*, so subtly sometimes that we do not even realise this is happening.

We should take notice that Jeremiah's account of the Queen of Heaven's influence over the children of Israel highlights their allegiance to her as the source of their provision:

16 "As for the word (message) that you have spoken to us in the name of the Lord, we are not going to listen to you. 17 But rather we will certainly perform every word of the vows we have made: to burn sacrifices to the queen of heaven (Ishtar) and to pour out drink offerings to her, just as we ourselves and our forefathers, our kings and our princes did in the cities of Judah and in the streets of Jerusalem; for [then] we had plenty of food and were prosperous and saw no misfortune."
Jeremiah 44: 16,17

This spirit has historically been able to effectively deceive God's people, causing them to be led astray, forsaking their faithful Father for the sake of abundant provision, drawing the whole family into the bondage of covenant as they relied upon her.

While we may not enter into open covenant with the Queen of Heaven for the sake of provision as the children of Israel did, as we disconnect from Jesus our Source and the certainty of the supernatural flow of provision and favour that can only come from Him, we are weakened and compromised as burdens of responsibility start to weigh heavily upon our shoulders that were never meant to be there.

We have already clearly seen in the previous chapter that a married couple rightly aligned in Christ has tremendous ability to prosper, whoever is the breadwinner, but we see the pervasive influence of this spirit's warfare against the 'head' when a woman is obliged to become the provider because the man is either unable to provide or has been disempowered in some way from doing so effectively.

That's the whole point. The Queen of Heaven will, wherever she has an opportunity, render the head ineffective.

Now that we have revelation of the Godly wisdom undergirding the Proverbs 31 marriage, as wives we can see to it that the head becomes powerfully effective as we surround our husbands and carry their hearts in the secret place before God, seeing them established in their Kingdom governmental position, experiencing a release of supernatural favour and provision that starts to break the stifling grip of this spirit's power.

We are to receive from Jesus as we remain connected to His headship and if we have disconnected in any way, becoming responsible for our own provision, then we have aligned to another source that is devoid of love. Self-sufficiency, striving and becoming exhausted by the effort of it all is the result. This is the cruel nature and hallmark of the Queen of Heaven's strategy against us: to intentionally pull us away from the Lord and subject us to the impossibility of providing for ourselves.

Whenever you are in a difficult financial situation and start to feel oppressed, lacking in faith and abandoned to the cares of this world, take notice. It is possible the Queen of Heaven is attempting to influence you.

In those moments, I pray that we will quickly discern the battle and step back into our rightful place, settling ourselves internally in the truth, that **Jesus** is our limit-less Source, consciously meditating upon the power of the connection we have with Him, until we feel the fear and the oppression break! The truth is that **Jesus** is responsible for our needs and we are to experience the joy and fulfilment of using our God-given abilities, dili-gently working with our hands to produce abiding fruit, as we rest in Him.

Jesus famously shared in John's Gospel:

"I am the Vine; you are the branches. The one who remains in Me and I in him bears much fruit, for (otherwise) apart from Me (that is, cut off from vital union with Me) you can do nothing." John 15: 5

This scripture has been gloriously fulfilled through our salvation. We have become a literal part of His Body and a permanent flow of limitless provision is now avail-able to us as we remain connected to the Head:

"Holding fast to the Head, from whom all the body, nourished and knit together by joints and ligaments, grows with the increase that is from God." Colossians 2:19

In Jesus we have the assurance of a God-given process of spiritual and financial growth at a pace that will enable to us to be established and bear fruit that will remain, as we *hold fast* to the Head.

As the manifestations of the work of the Queen of Heaven are revealed to us, the Holy Spirit is removing the veil that obscured our sight, equipping us to discern this spirit's ongoing efforts to influence God's people.

The absolute significance of Jesus' Headship, both personally and corporately, cannot be overstated. As we cleave to His Headship, take up our rightful place as His Body and refuse to give way, her influence over us will begin to break down, along with her schemes to weaken our ability to receive from Jesus all that was rightfully ours in the first place.

Pondering over all these things, seeing the ways in which I myself had subtly been affected, even as a spirit filled believer, I had to prayerfully ask the question, "How can a power like this gain access to our lives, our sexuality, our marriages, beyond ignorance of her schemes?" I received the simple answer: through open doors.

We are learning within the Body of Christ that wherever there are un-repented family ancestral covenants or any personal agreements that we have entered into, however innocently, an open door has been created.

We may also be confident that our own lives and the bloodline are free, yet if we live in an area where territorial rights have been granted over the land itself through covenant with the Queen of Heaven, ancient or current, she has a legal right to operate in the heavenlies and we are affected by her influence, whether we are personally free or not.

To have such understanding is a blessing because it will ensure we are no longer subject to an influence we know nothing of. As we prayerfully repent for any such alignment or covenant with the Queen of Heaven, we are certain of the victory that lies in Jesus' unfailing love and acceptance of us and the power of His blood to cleanse.

As we have seen, many are the ways in which we can unknowingly agree with this powerful, over-arching spirit, but our eyes are being opened and the ancient work of the Queen of Heaven is being exposed. Jesus is equipping us to break every agreement, moving in sufficient authority to uproot the legal rights that have empowered her, not only in our personal lives, but from the land and the nations of the earth.

Jesus is preparing His Bride... While it may appear that the call to know Him personally and intimately is only for the few, or for those who have time to devote themselves exclusively to such a wholehearted pursuit, actually this call is for every single one of us. The call to the intimate knowledge of Jesus is a master-stroke of genius.

The more we know Him, the more deeply we will become connected to Him, accessing everything that He is. As His strength flows into us, the more we become like Him and the more powerful we will become.

Intimacy is the ultimate strategic weapon.

We cannot be mastered by the realm of darkness because we have become wholly filled and flooded with God Himself, living and walking in the victory of the Cross. It is no wonder the enemy would come against our ability to walk in intimacy with Jesus, but we are learning to resist him and to press in, that we may receive the full measure of that which rightfully belongs to us!

As we respond to Jesus' invitation to know His heart and love Him, taking even small and tentative steps towards Him as I did, He will equip us for victory in battles of which we are, as yet, unaware.

I can now see that The Mantle of Purity was a vital and *strategic* gift because it provided supernatural empowerment to walk in the beauty of holiness and as my needs were met in Jesus, such freedom generated authority sufficient to withstand even the most subtle and deceptive work of the Queen of Heaven herself. How can we be snared to seek fulfilment outside of God's design when our needs are being fully met in Him?

The mantle was a personal gift but I knew, as Jesus placed it upon me, that this represented a shift for the Body of Christ, that even as His people are struggling in the deepest, most private parts of their lives, He has the answer. He is the answer and He is going to release this mantle of purity upon ALL who desire to receive it as supernatural empowerment that will free us from the most complex situation or intimate problem we may have.

Right now, even as you read these words and feel a longing in your heart to receive the Mantle of Purity, I pray for you in the Name of Jesus and impart to you all that I received of the holiness and purity of Jesus Himself and ask for even more healing and liberty to cascade throughout your entire being! We are called, as the

Bride of Christ, to take up the position of power that Jesus has given us:

"And [so that you can know and understand] what is the immeasurable and unlimited and surpassing greatness of His power in and for us who believe, as demonstrated in the working of His mighty strength, Which He exerted in Christ when He raised Him from the dead and seated Him at His [own] right hand in the heavenly [places], Far above all rule and authority and power and dominion and every name that is named [above every title that can be conferred], not only in this age and in this world, but also in the age and the world which are to come. And He put all things under His feet and has appointed Him the universal and supreme Head of the church [a headship exercised throughout the church], Which is His body, the fullness of Him Who fills all in all [for in that body lives the full measure of Him Who makes everything complete and Who fills everything everywhere with Himself" Ephesians 1: 19-23.

Let us absorb the incredible power of the meaning of this scripture!

Demonic powers may have sought to push us out of our rightful place, weakening the collective authority of the Body of Christ, exposing us and the society we live in to their pernicious influence, but our personal and corporate authority is being restored as we pursue Him and love Him with all our hearts.

As each one of us **becomes filled with the fullness of Him who fills and completes all things,** we will occupy our ascended position in the heavenlies and begin to rule.

It is *our* eternal destiny to rule as the Queen, of the King of Kings and we are being called in this hour to step into the fullness of our true identity, powerful, pure, holy and free!

THE SECOND EVE

The final revelation of Jesus' purpose in giving me the Mantle of Purity came as a dear friend sent me the newly published volumes of Frances Metcalfe's entire works as a gift. Since that winter's morning in Liz's kitchen almost three years earlier, I had not seen or read Frances' testimony that so moved my heart at that time, again.

Searching the pages eagerly, in Volume Two I found the wonderful story I was looking for. Savouring the words, I could hardly believe my eyes as the details of her profound encounter with Jesus unfolded for the second time, because I realised it had established in her the "grace of the pristine purity of Eve":

"I cried unto Him that morning with all the intensity of devotion of which God made me capable. And, suddenly, He appeared! When I say appeared, I mean just that. I saw Him! I touched Him! I talked with Him face to face, not as a King, not as a Creator, not as the Son of God, but, to my surprise, as the Son of Man! In condescension, my Lord came thus to me, in humility, in kindness, in tender love. As a man, I could approach

*him. I could draw very near Him and not be overawed.
I was shown how much He loves His office as Son of
Man. Indeed, He referred to Himself – as recorded in
the Gospels – by this name, more than by any other...*
**Yes, I saw Him as a man, as perfect Man, the Second
Adam. Not until I saw Him did I fully understand
what God had meant man, made in His image, to be.
Just a tender look from His eyes seemed to establish me
in the grace of the pristine purity of Eve before the fall.**
*I walked with Him through the dew-sprinkled morning.
As we walked, He talked with me and I lost all con-
sciousness of a world of sin, warring in violence. I
forgot that I was a mature, married woman, a mother
of children.* **I felt what St Paul meant when he said,
speaking of the Bride of Christ, "I have betrothed thee,
as a chaste virgin." The chastity and purity of true vir-
ginity were revealed to me that morning as I walked
with the One altogether pure. O, the beauty of the first
Eve! Praise God for the incorruptible beauty of the
second Eve – Bride of the Second Adam! This glorious
creature lived in me that morning! I was washed, puri-
fied, chaste and I was betrothed.** *This was all I knew,
all I could think of, all that mattered. Do you see that
for the moment I was portraying the Bride – indeed I
was lost in her and she was lost in Him...*[14]"

Absorbing the impact of Frances' testimony, I finally
understood what had happened to me. As Jesus placed
His Mantle upon my shoulders He had established me
in the grace of the pristine purity of Eve, before the fall.

---

[14] Excerpt from 'Ladies of Gold' Volume 2, page 31-32 by James
Maloney, © Answering the Cry Publications, Westbow Press

How can this be possible?

In His office as the 'Son of Man' Jesus became a man, completely identifying with us in our humanity: "The first man [Adam] is from the earth, earthy [made of dust]; the second Man [Christ, the Lord] is from heaven. As is the earthly man [the man of dust], so are those who are of earth; and as is the heavenly [Man], so are those who are of heaven." 1 Corinthians 15: 47,48

Those of us who are 'of heaven', who are born again of the Spirit, **have access to the perfection of humanity that is in Jesus Himself.**

As the 'last' Adam, He is the perfect man, the perfection of mankind, for all eternity. He paid the price as the perfect sacrifice to *fully* redeem us, the power of His blood reaching all the way back to what happened in the Garden of Eden. In Him and through Him, as men and women that have been 'born again', we have the opportunity therefore to carry afresh the original mandates for male and female given to Adam and Eve.

To be *with* Him is the key to the depths of this profound miracle. Frances literally spent time with Jesus and was profoundly, indelibly touched. Decades later as He physically came to me, Jesus' Presence was so indescribably beautiful and powerful that the nobility of my gender as He originally created it to be was immediately brought forth in my life, as it was for Frances Metcalfe.

From the moment the encounter receded I knew I had been wonderfully blessed, but as I now read

Frances' testimony again, my eyes were opened still further to receive the revelation that as we are in His Presence, the impact of the fall of man is more deeply removed from our lives.

Jesus has utterly defeated sin and death and when we are with Him, time and the realities of this world lose their apparent hold on us. It is impossible to be physically with Him and not be filled with the manifestation of that which He has spoken about us, about mankind, from the foundation of the earth.

As we are with Him, we are in the eternal realm, receiving the perfection of His Divine Nature in the very depths of our being. As we are with Him, the One who is the Word made flesh, who is holding everything together by the power of the Word, who is the Truth, the Life, the Way, touches the very core of our DNA to bring it in line with the truth of who we *really* are and what we have been mandated to do, for His Glory.

We would be wise to pursue the presence of Jesus Himself, to make Him the priority of our lives, as with just one touch He can restore us in ways we did not dream possible.

In just a few most sacred moments with Him, with one sovereign gift of a silver mantle of purity, Jesus revealed to me the depth of the redeeming work of the Cross, proving to me that His blood is sufficient not only to bring His People forth in shining glory as the Bride, but as the pinnacle of the Created Order itself. A noble people, holy and wise, to whom the creation itself will respond.

Jesus desires to restore *each one of us*, both men and women. Genesis 1:27 tells us that God created man in His own image:

> *"So God created man in His own image;*
> *In the image and likeness of God He created him;*
> *male and female He created them."*

From the very beginning, as men and women we were created to literally reflect the glory of God Himself. It is this glory that is being restored to us. We were made to be like Him...

In the same way therefore that Jesus' purity returned me to the glory of the womanhood of Eve, a 'second' Eve, Jesus wants to do the same for the men, as a type of the 'second' Adam. I have seen the place of perfect manhood in Jesus and it can be accessed! Frances said, "Not until I saw Him did I fully understand what God had meant man, made in His image, to be."

The glory of perfect manhood is *in* Jesus and as men, pursuing His Presence as the deer that pants for water, Jesus will meet with you. The glory of the Divine Nature, the glory of His manhood and the beauty of His image can shine forth from your life. The strength and order the world is crying out for will be released as you begin to walk in the glory of manhood as He originally intended!

Frances Metcalfe and 'The Golden Candlestick', the group of fervent, powerful intercessors who knew themselves as the Bride, interceded for decades in the isolated mountain-top town of Idyllwild, California. They had an extraordinary ministry powerfully focused on Jesus, experiencing an unprecedented realm of encounter, praying in faith for the Bride of Christ to come forth in future generations. That is why there is such a mighty impartation upon the word of their testimony, captured in Frances' writings. They prayed that the depth of their experience in God would somehow spur others on to desire the same for themselves and their prophetic intercession is being fulfilled in our day as the Company of the Bride is coming forth.

From glory to glory I came to know Jesus, through the power of my salvation as a young girl, the baptism of the Holy Spirit, treasuring the vital ongoing ministry of the Spirit, the years of wonderful adventures, pursuing Jesus through the mountaintop experiences and the painful valleys, even of the shadow of death. All led to the day when my eyes were finally opened and I saw Him at last, face to face.

The scriptures declare,

> *"Blessed are the pure in heart, for they*
> *shall see God"* Matthew 5: 8 NKJV.

Jesus sees the sincerity of our efforts to love and know Him, imperfect as we are and the offering of our heart is pure to Him. It is this that moves His heart, it is so precious to Him that for this reason He is willing to reveal Himself in return. The promised blessing, that our eyes will then be opened and **we shall see God,** is ours.

Never, ever underestimate the value of the way you love Jesus or the ways in which you have faithfully followed Him, for they will lead to the fulfilment of this promise in your life, in the perfection of His timing. He is faithful and He will give you the desires of your heart.

In February 2015, I had a powerful dream where I was standing in the sea, to the depth of about three feet. Just a short distance away, the Apostle Peter was being baptized. There was an angel standing behind him.

As Peter went down the Holy Spirit came into the water, He was swirling round and round Peter in a blaze of fire and golden light and so much power was being released that it felt like fire in the very depths of my being. The power of what was happening became so strong it lifted Peter up out of the water, he was taken up high and then placed on a solid rock which was so enormous that as you looked, it then spread out to become land that reached as far as the eye could see. Peter had been placed on the immoveable and enduring foundation of Jesus Himself.

In the dream, the Spirit's incredible ministry around Peter as he was lifted out of the sea to stand on the Rock was so vivid and real that I was touched by the same power. As the force of this anointing hit my spirit, the Holy Spirit showed me what He is doing: we are being re-commissioned to fulfil the original mandate given in Matthew 16: 13-18:

"When Jesus came into the region of Caesarea Philippi, He asked His disciples, saying "Who do

men say that I, the Son of Man, am?" So they said, "Some say John the Baptist, some Elijah and others Jeremiah or one of the prophets." He said to them, "but who do you say that I am?" Simon Peter answered and said, "You are the Christ, the Son of the living God." Jesus answered and said to him, "Blessed are you Simon Bar-Jonah, for flesh and blood has not revealed this to you, but My Father who is in Heaven. And I also say to you that you are Peter and on this rock I will build My church, and the gates of Hades shall not prevail against it." NKJV

Jesus and Jesus alone is the Rock, the undergirding foundation of the Ekklesia. Baptized in the Spirit, Peter received power to faithfully lay this foundation over and over again, never faltering from the work he was given to do, dying a martyr's death because of His love for the Son of God.

The dream is illuminating the powerful reality that as *we* stand on Jesus as the only Rock and Foundation, baptized in the power of the Holy Spirit, Jesus will establish His Ekklesia in and through us! No matter what we are called to do, Jesus is the only foundation of that work and He will extend His Kingdom through us.

It is powerful to realise that the greater the personal revelation of Jesus we have, of His love and power to absolutely transform our lives, cities, nations, even the creation itself, the greater the depth of foundation will be set in place. *Only* that which is built on Jesus will endure and remain:

"For no other foundation can anyone lay than that which is laid, which is Jesus Christ. Now if anyone builds on this foundation with gold, silver, precious stones, wood, hay, straw, each one's work will become clear; for the Day will declare it, because it will be revealed by fire; and the fire will test each one's work, of what sort it is"
1 Corinthians 3: 11-13

This is the way the Holy Spirit is leading in this hour. At a time when incredible vision and hope for transformation on every level is being released to the Body of Christ, the Spirit is bringing about a powerful and profound alignment, leading us to pursue depths of relationship with Jesus until we know His heart, until we have become like Him, fully satisfied in Him, governmental like Him and then, the gates of Hell will not be able to prevail against us. We will transform every sphere of society as His powerful presence dwells in us and flows out of the very fibre of our being.

Our relationship with Jesus is a powerful, wonderful gift that will go to deeper depths and higher heights as we continue to pursue Him. Our life in Him has incredible meaning. As we fulfil every God-given vision, it is our destiny to bring the transforming love and presence of Jesus Christ right into the heart of the world we live in. Together, may we carry His Presence to the utter ends of the earth.

JULIE BROWN

Julie Brown has served in ministry for over 20 years. As a fourth generation Christian, born again and set apart in the fire of the Holy Spirit's ministry, she is called to know the heart of the Lamb and to proclaim the truths that He reveals.

As co-Founder and Director of 'The Bridal Company', Julie has the privilege of serving alongside Liz Wright to instil within the Body of Christ the understanding of who we are as the Bride, made in the image of God, reigning with Him!

With over 20 years' experience in prophetic intercession, Julie is also called as a seer and strategist, receiving revelation for breakthrough in prayer, serving leaders and the Transformation movement with those strategies, at a local, national and international level.

Her second book, 'Polished Arrow' © will share powerful insights and strategies for anointed, prophetic intercession, available early 2019.

Julie lives with her family in the beautiful County of Lincolnshire, United Kingdom.

Lightning Source UK Ltd.
Milton Keynes UK
UKHW01f0241170518
322674UK00001B/47/P